☆ CHEER SPIRIT ☆

MAKE SOME NOISE

Cheers and Chants that Fire Up the Crowd

by Rebecca Rissman

Consultant:
Tara L. Wieland
Owner and Head Coach
Michigan Storm Cheer and Dance
Midland, Michigan

CAPSTONE PRESS
a capstone imprint

Snap Books are published by Capstone Press,
1710 Roe Crest Drive, North Mankato, Minnesota 56003
www.capstonepub.com

Library of Congress Cataloging-in-Publication Data
Rissman, Rebecca.
  Make some noise : chants and cheers that fire up the crowd / by Rebecca
Rissman.
     pages cm. — (Cheer Spirit)
  Includes webography.
  Includes bibliographical references and index.
    Audience: Age: 8-14.
  ISBN 978-1-4914-5204-2 (library binding)
  ISBN 978-1-4914-5220-2 (eBook PDF)
  1. Cheers—Juvenile literature. I. Title.
  LB3635.R57 2015
  791.6′4—dc23
                        2015009411

Editorial Credits
Abby Colich, editor; Heidi Thompson, designer; Tracy Cummins, media
researcher; Katy LaVigne, production specialist

Photo Credits
AP Photo: Phelan M. Ebenhack, 17; Capstone Press: Karon Dubke, Cover,
6, 14-15, 21; Getty Images: Bill Frakes/Sports Illustrated, 29, J. Meric, 23,
Jonathan Daniel, 22; iStockphoto: stevecoleimages, 5; Shutterstock: Aspen
Photo, 8 Bottom, 13, 24, 27 Top, 30, bikeriderlondon, 18, Monkey Business
Images, 10, Robert Adrian Hillman, Design Element, Sebastian Kaulitzki, 7,
surachet khamsuk, Design Element, SUSAN LEGGETT, 27 Bottom, zsooofija

Design Element; Thinkstock: Mike Powell, 8-9

Printed in the United States of America in North Mankato, Minnesota.
052015   008823CGF15

TABLE OF CONTENTS

"CAN YOU HEAR ME?"

Cheerleaders often wow the crowd with amazing flips and jumps. But cheerleaders do so much more. A cheerleader's most important job is to pump up the fans. After all, what team can resist the sound of a roaring crowd? If you know when to use the right cheers and chants, you'll be sure to boost everyone's spirits.

CHEERS

Cheerleaders lead the crowd in both cheers and chants. Cheers are usually longer, rhyming rallying calls to the crowd. They are often done during a break in the game's action, such as halftime or a time-out. Doing cheers when the athletes aren't playing means that the crowd can listen and enjoy. Some cheerleading squads use dance moves, stunts, or gymnastics during their cheers.

CHANTS

Chants are similar to cheers, but they are usually shorter. Cheerleaders encourage the crowds to repeat their chants many times in a row. Chants can be done while the game is being played.

CHEER TIP!

When the crowd cheers along, it boosts the athletes' spirits. Your cheers could help lead the players to win the game!

LET'S GET LOUD!

Clear your throat and take a deep breath. Get ready to shout! Whether you're on a cheerleading squad or in the stands, you need to be loud, clear, and enthusiastic. Here are a few tricks to make sure your cheers are heard.

CHEER TIP!

Being loud is only part of a great cheer. The crowd must also understand what you are saying. On the sidelines or in the stands, always speak clearly when cheering. Practicing tongue twisters will help sharpen your speech. With fans, game action, the band, and other noise, a clear voice is a must!

Finding Your Diaphragm

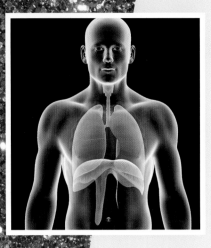

The diaphragm is an organ between your chest and stomach. It helps you breathe. It is important to know how to use your diaphragm when shouting cheers. Using your diaphragm will help make your voice louder. It will also protect your vocal chords. To find your diaphragm, lie down on your back. Place one hand on your stomach. Take a deep breath in and then push it out quickly. Then say, "Ho! Ho! Ho!" You should be able to feel your diaphragm working. Next, take a deep breath. Watch your belly rise up as you do. Doing slow deep breathing exercises, such as this one, will strengthen your diaphragm and help you cheer more loudly.

Get low. Don't let the pitch, or tone, of your voice get too high. If you scream, your cheers will be difficult to understand. Instead, try to shout in a lower pitch.

Be clear. Pronounce your words clearly. It helps to emphasize consonant sounds, such as T, P, D, and B.

Stick to the beat. Following a rhythm will help you and your fellow cheerleaders stay in sync as you cheer.

Clap and stomp. Don't just rely on your voice! Remember that you can use your hands and feet to be heard too.

7

GET MUSICAL!

A pep band is a small musical group that plays instruments during games and pep rallies. Cheerleading squads sometimes create routines to go with songs the pep band plays. Seeing the cheerleaders dance while the pep band plays the school fight song really gets the crowd excited.

TEAM UP!

Spice up your cheers with music and crowd participation. Many cheerleading squads involve a team mascot in their routines. Mascots can dance along to cheerleading routines with a pair of pom-poms. Crowds always love this new addition to the squad.

When to cheer or chant:

★ when the team scores
★ when the team is on the field, mat, or court
★ after a good play
★ when player substitutions are made
★ when your team is down and needs encouragement
★ before the game, during time-outs, and halftime

When NOT to cheer or chant:

★ when a player is injured
★ when a referee is making a call

THE BEST CHANTS

What's the difference between a good cheer and a great cheer? Just listen to the crowd to find out. Fans love cheering, clapping, and stomping along to fun and exciting cheers and chants. The louder the crowd, the better the cheer!

Great chants are catchy, rhythmic, and rhyme. They are also easy for fans to learn quickly and remember. Chants with a strong rhythm and rhyme are simple to follow.

Regardless of the sport, involving the crowd makes cheers and chants fun. Call and response cheers are a great way to do this. Cheerleaders call out a phrase, and the crowd either repeats their call or shouts their response. Try the following example of a call and response chant using your school color.

Cheerleaders: I say "GO BIG!" You say "BLUE!"
Cheerleaders: GO BIG!
Crowd: BLUE!
Cheerleaders: GO BIG!
Crowd: BLUE!

A longer cheer, such as this one, can be performed with movements during a time-out or halftime.

Hey you Cougar fans,

Come on and clap your hands!

Now stomp your feet,

When you've got the beat!

When you feel the groove,

Just start to move!

So have no fear!

It's time to cheer!

Let's hear you yell!

Let's hear you shout!

Let's hear you hoot!

And belt it out!

Let's hear it for the Cougars!

The Cougars are the best!

Let's hear it for the Cougars!

They're better than the rest!

SCHOOL COLORS

Use colors in your cheers. If your school or cheer team's colors are red and blue, think of words that rhyme with blue, such as "true" and "you."

Watch out! Watch out!

We are the red and blue.

Watch out! Watch out!

We're coming for you.

Watch out! Watch out!

You know it's true!

MASCOT AND TEAM NAME

Cheers often include a team name or mascot. For example, if your team mascot is the Bluejay or Eagle, include words such as "fly" and "soar."

Eagles fly!

Eagles soar!

Eagles fight!

Eagles score!

CHEER TIP!

Be creative! Try to think of fun, unique rhymes that the crowd would enjoy.

FOOTBALL CHEERS AND CHANTS

Each sport is different. Different cheers and chants are needed for each sport. Some cheers and chants are used just for football. During football games, cheerleaders need to be loud! Outdoor football stadiums are often large and windy, so cheerleaders need to work hard to be heard. Try some of these football chants and see how loud you can be.

Let's score!

(stomp stomp)

Let's score!

(stomp stomp)

Score and let's get six points more!

First down!

First down!

On our way to a TOUCHDOWN!

Defense

✴ (clap clap) ✴

Defense

✴ (clap clap) ✴

SCORE!

In football there are different ways to score. Knowing the rules for scoring will help you know which cheer to use at the right time. A touchdown earns the team 6 points. An extra point attempt can happen after a touchdown. It can earn the team 1 or 2 points. A field goal earns the team 3 points. When a team is playing offense, they are trying to score. When they are playing defense, they are trying to stop their opponents from scoring.

KNOW THE FIELD!

Learn the parts of a football field and include them in your cheers and chants. A football field has two end zones. These are the areas between the goal line and the end line. Players can score touchdowns by catching the ball inside of the end zone, or by running with the ball into the end zone. Try these chants the next time you need to boost your favorite football team's spirits.

End zone!
Here we come!
End zone!
We're number one!

Feel the heat!
Yeah, feel the heat.
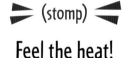 (stomp)
Feel the heat!
We can't be beat!
(clap)

Grab that pigskin,
✳ (clap clap clap) ✳
Drive it home,
✳ (clap clap clap) ✳
Run that pigskin
✳ (clap clap clap) ✳
To the zone!

Learn common football terms and slang. Footballs are made from leather. A common nickname for a football is "pigskin." "Sack" is a common football term for a tackle.

KNOW THE PLAYERS

In football there are several positions. The quarterback is the team leader. He calls the plays and catches the ball at the beginning of each play. The kicker kicks field goals. Linebackers and defensive tackles block and tackle members of the opposite team. The following chants provide ways to include specific football players.

Our kicker's here!
So have no fear!
His magic feet
Just can't be beat!
He'll give it his all!
He's ready to roll!
He'll send that ball
Right through your goal!

Our quarterback
He is the best!
Our quarterback
Is better than the rest!
Our quarterback
Will win this game!
Our quarterback
You know his name!
LET'S GO, [player's name]!
LET'S GO, [player's name]!

CHEER TIP!

Pay attention to the game. Lead the crowd in cheers for offense, defense, extra point attempts, field goals, and touchdowns.

BASKETBALL CHEERS AND CHANTS

Other cheers and chants are used just at basketball games. Basketball cheers need to be short, loud, and energetic. Try making these fun cheers and chants your own by adding motions, stomps, and crowd participation.

The hoop!
The hoop!
Drive it to the hoop!
Yeah, yeah, yeah!

Lay up!
Lay up!
Get down!
Get down!
We're the best!
We're the best!
Team in town!

SCORE!

Basketball players can score 1, 2, or 3 points at a time. A free throw earns 1 point. A basket earns 2 points. And a basket thrown from outside the three-point line earns 3 points. Some of the ways to shoot have different names. A layup is a basket thrown from below the hoop. Players who can dunk jump high and put the ball into the basket with their hands. Knowing what's happening during the game will help you know when to cheer and chant and which ones to use.

Fire up the crowd with this longer cheer during a time-out or halftime.

Our girls are going to take the floor.
They are the players you adore.
One and two and three and four!
Our team is going to score, score, score!

Our girls are going to take the floor.
They're going to SWOOSH for two points more!
One and two and three and four!
You fans are going to roar, roar, roar!

Our girls are going to take the floor!
Our opponents will run straight for the door!
One and two and three and four!
We'll fight and win this basketball war!

KNOW THE SPORT

The more you know about the sport you are cheering for, the more cheers and chants you'll be able to create. In basketball players can dribble, pass, or shoot the ball. If a player moves his or her feet while keeping the ball in hand, it is called traveling. The other team will get the ball. Just like in football, in basketball offense is when a team has the possession of the ball and is trying to score. Defense is when they are trying to stop the other team from scoring. Try adding some of these terms into your basketball cheers, or use the following examples.

Get two!
Get two!
You know what to do—SWOOSH!
(Repeat three times.)

Watch her dribble!
Watch her run!
Watch her shoot!
She's number one!

Dribble, shoot, shoot!
Take that ball to the hoop, hoop!

Sink it!
Score it!
Two points more!
✳ (clap) ✳
(Repeat three times.)

Always Improve

If you are on a cheerleading squad, ask your coach if you can take turns sitting out during practice. Watch and listen to your squad. Can you understand all the words in the cheers? If not, think of ways your team can be clearer. Work on the parts of cheers that were difficult to understand.

GETTING THE BALL

When a team isn't trying to score, they are trying to get the ball from the other team. Players can get the ball from the other team in different ways. They can catch a ball that bounces off the basket in a rebound. Or they can steal the ball from a member of the opposite team. With so much action in this sport, it's easy to find cheers and chants for every move.

R-E-B-O-U-N-D
Let's get that rebound
1, 2, 3!

Woah, it just got real!

Did you see that steal?

It just got real!

Did you see that steal?

Let's go, Ravens!

Take it to the hoop!

Let's go, Ravens!

Throw 'em for a loop!

. . . .

On your mark!

Get set!

Shoot that ball right through that net!

(Repeat three times.)

Give it

* (clap clap) *

Your all!

* (clap clap) *

Let's rebound

* (clap clap) *

That ball!

* (clap clap) *

Drink Up! How to Stay Hydrated on Game Day

Staying hydrated is important for any athlete. But it's especially important for an athlete who needs to cheer and shout to an excited crowd. Cheerleaders need to drink plenty of water to make sure they are ready to be LOUD.

★ Drink at least eight glasses of water each day.

★ Bring a bottle of water to the game with you.

★ Avoid sugary drinks such as soda, juice, or sports drinks.

★ Avoid caffeinated drinks.

★ If you drink milk, choose low-fat or nonfat options.

WRESTLING CHEERS AND CHANTS

Cheering at a wrestling meet presents a unique challenge. Cheerleaders have to get the crowd pumped up—while sitting down! In this sport, one participant tries to take control of the other on a mat. Because wrestlers are so close to the ground, cheerleaders sit on the floor. This allows everyone to see the action. These cheerleaders use their voices, hands, and feet to energize the wrestlers to do their best. Try these chants at the next wrestling meet.

Ride 'em!
Roll 'em!
GET THAT PIN!
Ride 'em!
Roll 'em!
WIN! WIN! WIN!

. . . .

1, 2, 3, 4!
Pin him, pin him
To the floor!

Never give up!
⚡ (pound pound) ⚡
Never give in!
⚡ (pound pound) ⚡
Never give up!
⚡ (pound pound) ⚡
GET THAT PIN!

What do we want?
A pin!
What do we want?
A WIN!

. . . .

Go for the takedown!
If you wanna win,
Go for the takedown!
Pin! Pin! Pin!

PIN!

Wrestlers try to pin, or take down, their opponents. A pin is when one player forces another player onto his back. In order to count as a pin, both of the opponent's shoulders must be touching the mat for two seconds. Cheer for your wrestlers to get that pin!

GET THE RHYTHM! GET THE BEAT!

Some wrestling cheers don't have any words. Cheerleaders use their hands to pound the mat, and clasp and clap in exciting, drumlike rhythms. By pounding, rumbling, clapping, and slapping the mat in different ways, cheerleaders can get wrestlers and their fans pumped up.

Twist him like a pretzel!
Show him how you wrestle!
Pin him like a pretzel!
GET THAT WIN!

. . . .

Hey! Hey!
All right! All right!
Pin 'em! Pin 'em!
Pin 'em tonight!

P-I-N him to the mat!
P-I-N him!
PIN HIM FLAT!

. . . .

Go, [player's name]!
Fight, fight, fight!
Go, [player's name]!
Get a pin tonight!

CHEER TIP!

Be a good sport. You might hear cheers from the crowd that are negative or that encourage the other team to do poorly. Just ignore these. Encourage the crowd to participate in a positive cheer instead. Try to be a good role model with your positive spirit.

Clasp and Clap

To clap, cheerleaders make their hands flat and quickly bring their palms together. To clasp, they make a slightly cupped shape with their hands and bring their curved hands together. This makes a different noise from a clap.

CREATE YOUR OWN CHEER

Now that you've read about what makes a great cheer, it's time to make one of your own. Follow these steps to create a cheer that will pump up the crowd and rally your team to victory.

1. Use your team name, colors, mascot, or other symbol. For example, one team name might be the "Fighting Tigers."

2. Find a rhyme. Think of several words about your team's mascot that rhyme. Here are some examples of ways to include tigers in rhymes:

> Orange and black!
>
> Let's attack!
>
> ·
>
> Hear us roar!
>
> We're going to score!
>
> ·
>
> Razor sharp claws
>
> and terrifying jaws!

3. Make your cheer sport specific. For example, try adding some basketball terms such as

> score, shoot, dribble, or steal.

4. Put it together. Your cheer could be something like this:

> We are the Tigers!
>
> Hear us roar!
>
> Shoot that ball!
>
> We're going to score!
>
> ·
>
> We are the Tigers!
>
> We've got terrifying jaws!
>
> We'll shred that basket!
>
> With our razor sharp claws!

5. Take it to the next level. Add claps, stomps, and other movements.

6. Show it off. Perform your new cheer at your next practice. Have fun and try your best.

READ MORE

Hunt, Sara R. *You've Got Spirit: Cheers, Chants, Tips, and Tricks Every Cheerleader Needs to Know*. Minneapolis: Millbrook Press, 2013.

Webb, Margaret. *Pump It Up Cheerleading*. Sports Starters. New York: Crabtree Publishing, 2012.

Webber, Rebecca. *Varsity's Ultimate Guide to Cheerleading*. New York: Little, Brown, and Company, 2014.

Welsh, Piper. *Cheerleading*. Fun Sports for Fitness. Vero Beach, Fl.: Rourke Educational Media, 2013.

INTERNET SITES

FactHound offers a safe, fun way to find Internet sites related to this book. All of the sites on FactHound have been researched by our staff.

Here's all you do:

Visit *www.facthound.com*

Type in this code: 9781491452042

INDEX